DOWN ON THE FARM

by Merrily Kutner
illustrated by Will Hillenbrand

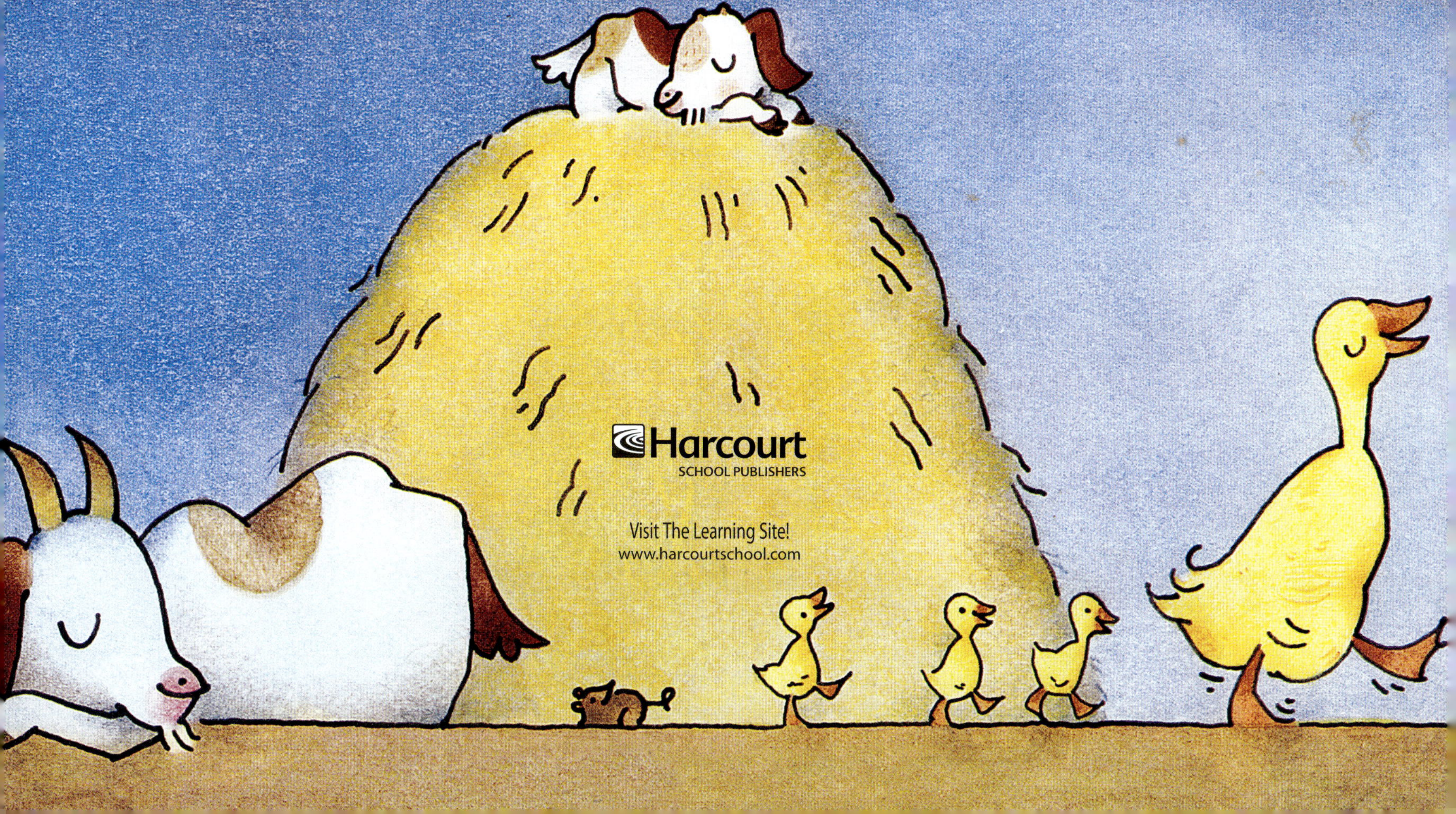

Harcourt
SCHOOL PUBLISHERS

Visit The Learning Site!
www.harcourtschool.com

This edition is published by special arrangement with Holiday House, Inc.

Grateful acknowledgment is made to Holiday House, Inc. for permission to reprint
Down on the Farm by Merrily Kutner, illustrated by Will Hillenbrand. Text copyright
© 2004 by Merrily Kutner; illustrations copyright © 2004 by Will Hillenbrand.

Printed in China

ISBN 10 0-15-352454-5
ISBN 13 978-0-15-352454-7

2 3 4 5 6 7 8 9 10 985 15 14 13 12 11 10 09 08 07

For my precious daughter, Marisa—
in loving memory
M. K.

To Sheri Woodward,
down on the farm
W. H.

4

Sun comes up.
Kid wakes up!
Down on the farm,
DOWN ON THE FARM.

"Rooster, shoo!"
Cock-a-doodle-doo.

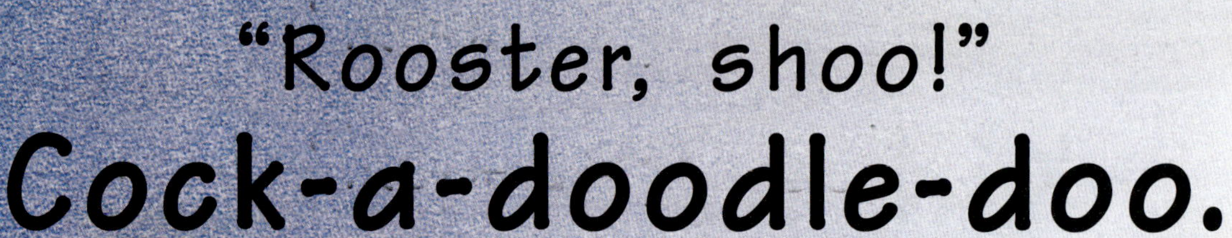

Down on the farm,
DOWN ON THE FARM.

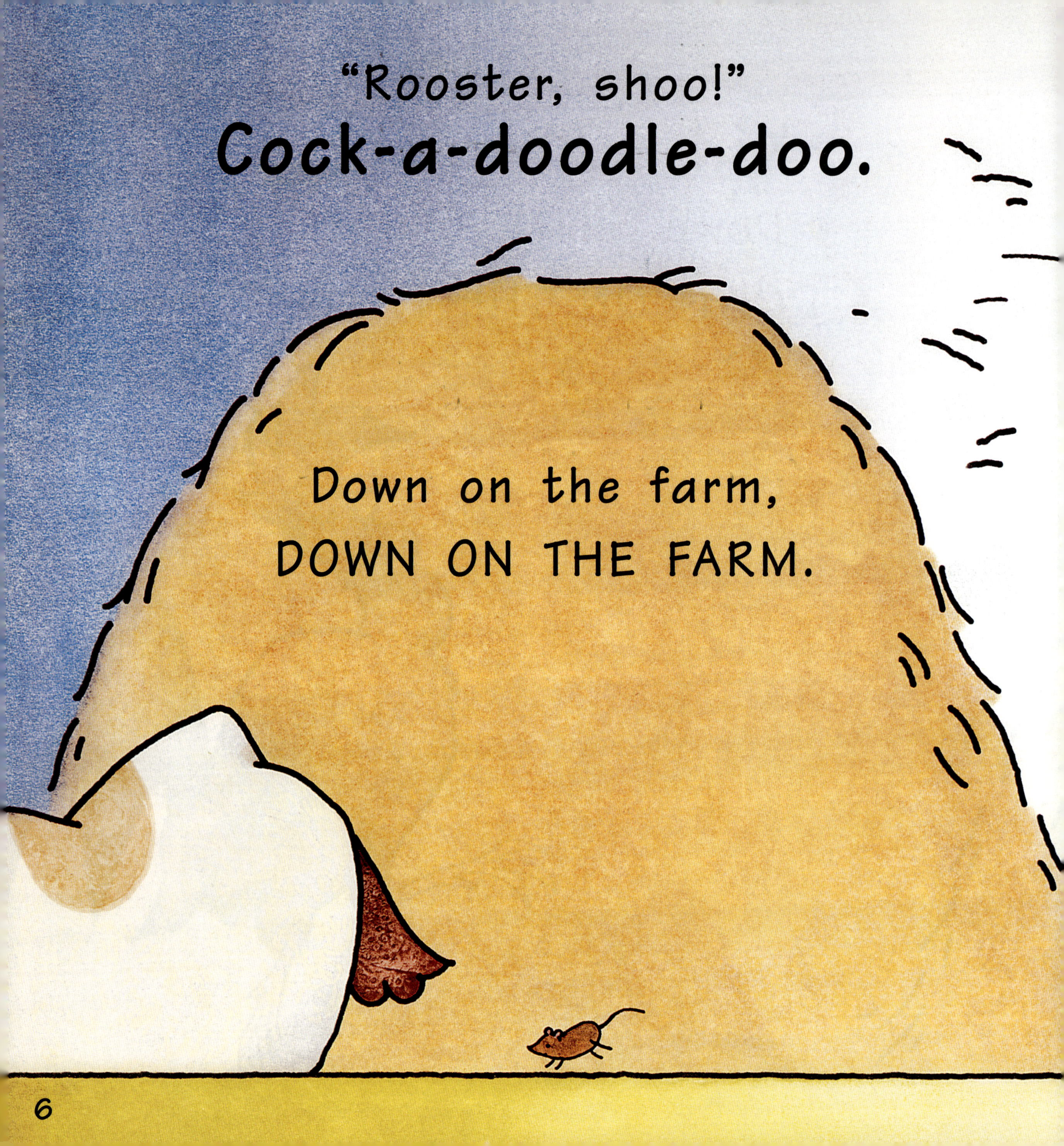

Crows peck straw—
Caw, caw, caw.
Down on the farm,
DOWN ON THE FARM.

Horses say,
"Nay, nay, nay."
Down on the farm,
DOWN ON THE FARM.

Cows will chew—
Moo, moo, moo.
Down on the farm,
DOWN ON THE FARM.

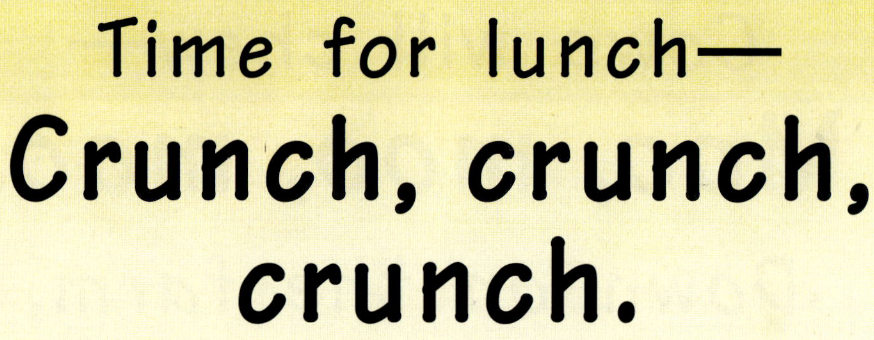

Time for lunch—
Crunch, crunch, crunch.
Down on the farm,
DOWN ON THE FARM.

12

"Ducks, come back!"
Quack, quack, quack.
Down on the farm,
DOWN ON THE FARM.

Geese kerplonk—
Honk, honk, honk.
Down on the farm,
DOWN ON THE FARM.

Turkeys squabble—
Gobble, gobble, gobble.
Down on the farm,
DOWN ON THE FARM.

Dog's on roof—
Woof, woof, woof.
Down on the farm,
DOWN ON THE FARM.

Pig snouts point—
Oink, oink, oink.
Down on the farm,
DOWN ON THE FARM.

Goats repeat,
"Bleat, bleat, bleat."
Down on the farm,
DOWN ON THE FARM.

Sheep graze far—
Baa, baa, baa.

Down on the farm,
DOWN ON THE FARM.

Chicks won't sleep—
Peep, peep, peep.
Down on the farm,
DOWN ON THE FARM.

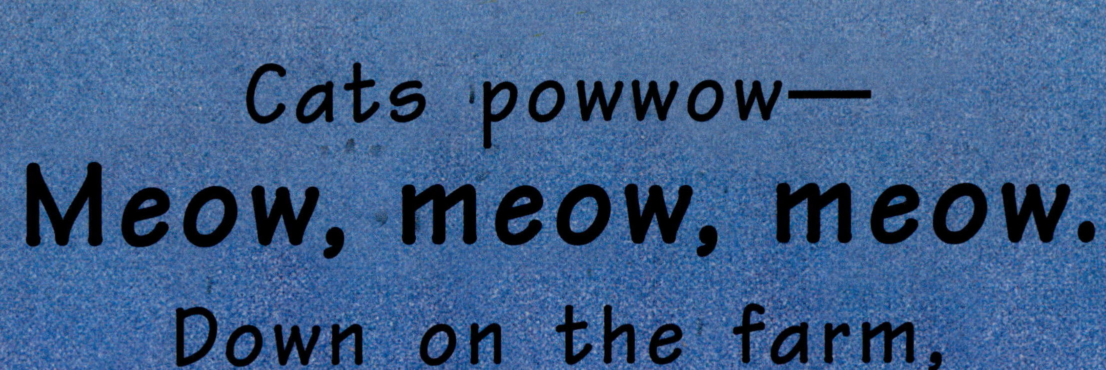

Cats powwow—
Meow, meow, meow.
Down on the farm,
DOWN ON THE FARM.

Sun goes down.
SHH!
Quiet town.
Down on the farm,
DOWN ON
THE FARM.